MW00901167

My
First
Book of
Catholic
Pictures

Michele E. Chronister
© 2018

Genre: [Catholic Liturgy] [Catechesis]

Summary: a pictorial guide to various items, vestments and vessels used in the Roman Catholic Mass

ISBN-13: 978-1548202354
ISBN-10: 1548202355

Another My Domestic Monastery publication. For more info, visit: http://www.mydomesticmonastery.com

This book is dedicated to my husband, Andrew, who shares my love for the Mass, for my children (Therese, Maria, Gabriel, and Zelie), my godchildren (Rosie, Arabella, Johnny, Louis, Michael, Max, Nina, Hero, and Rico), Dr. David Fagerberg (who gave me a love for the Theology of the Mass), and to the wonderful priests and seminarians at Kenrick-Glennon Seminary – I loved the Mass and the Sacraments from the time I was a child, but your dedication to the Liturgy makes me love it more than ever before. Thank you for giving God your "yes."

Special thanks to my fellow liturgy loving friends on Facebook for their advice and wisdom.

Introduction

From the time that I was a very small child, I loved the Mass. When I was old enough to become an altar server, and then later a lector, EM, and sacristan, I fell in love with the sacristy. I loved learning the names of the sacred vessels, loved seeing the closetful of the priest's chasubles, and I loved learning more about the symbolism and meaning behind each of the things that I saw at Mass.

Now as a mother, I see my children have the same interest and inquisitiveness.
There is a value to us knowing the names of things, in understanding the rich symbolism of our Catholic faith. The Catholic faith is a tangible, rich experience for the senses. Our Church is steeped in Sacramentals and Sacraments – in fragrant oils and beautiful images, in silken fabrics and in rising incense. The human being is created to encounter the world and to come to know God through the senses!

A companion to the *Catholic Field Guide*, this edition is intended for the young child, as he or she learns the names of what is seen at Mass.

-Michele E. Chronister

Ablution Cup

Alb

Altar

Altar Bells

Altar Cloth

Ambo

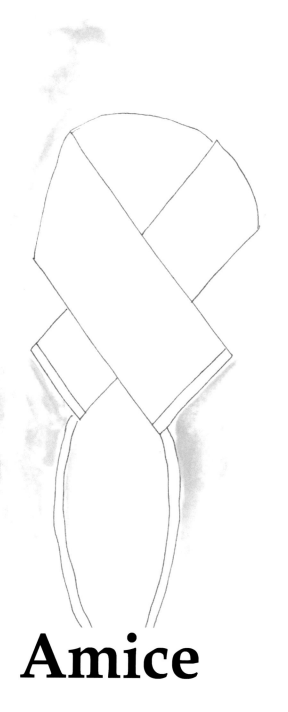

Amice

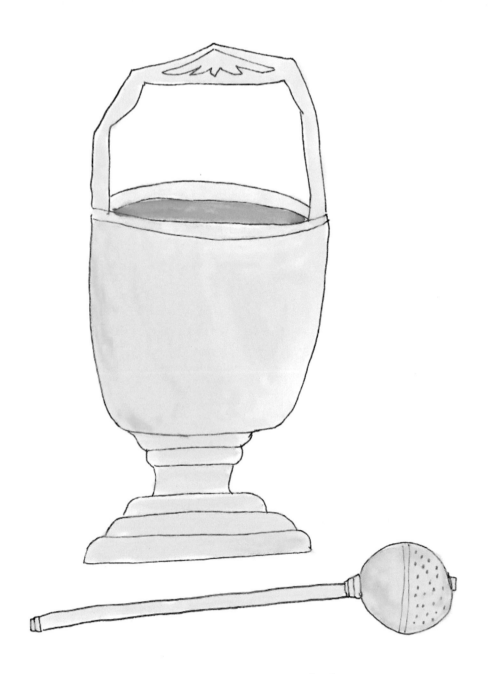

Aspergillum

Baldacchino

Baptismal Font

Baptismal Shell

Biretta

Book of the Gospels

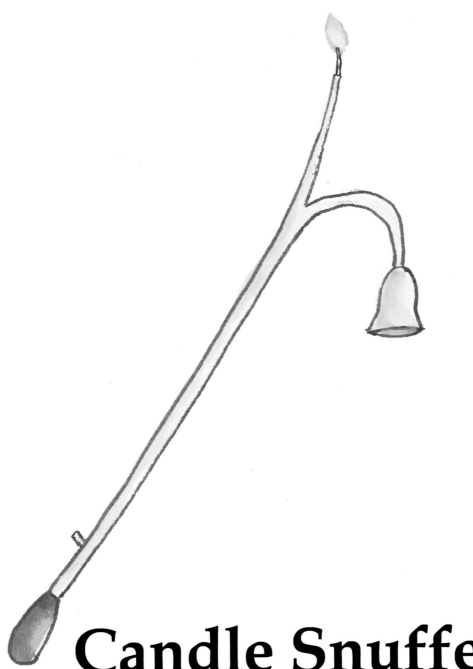

Candle Snuffer

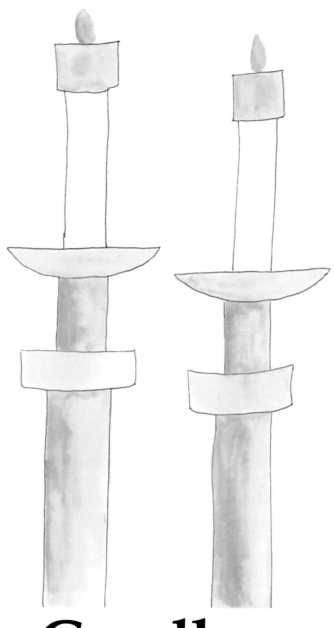

Candles

Cassock

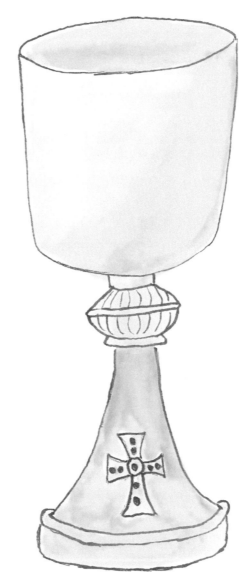

Chalice

Chalice Pall

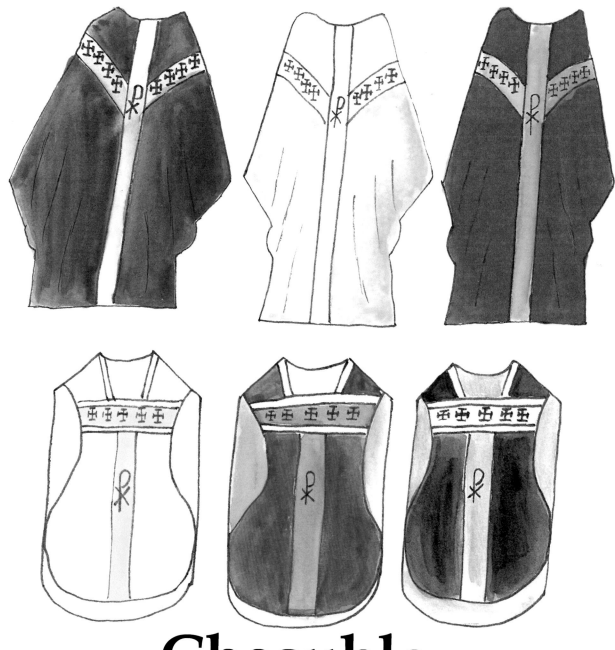

Chasuble

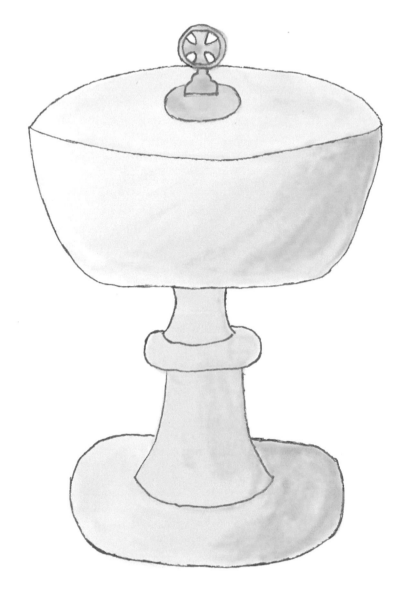

Ciborium

Cincture

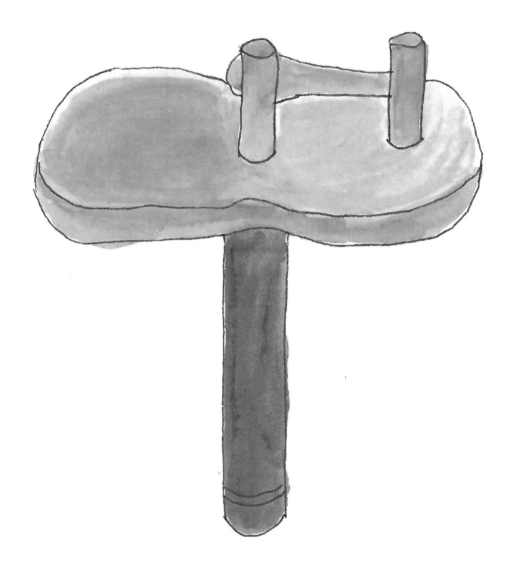

Clacker

Confessional

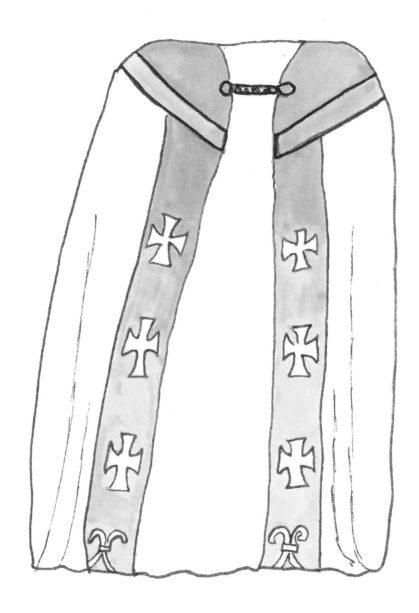

Cope

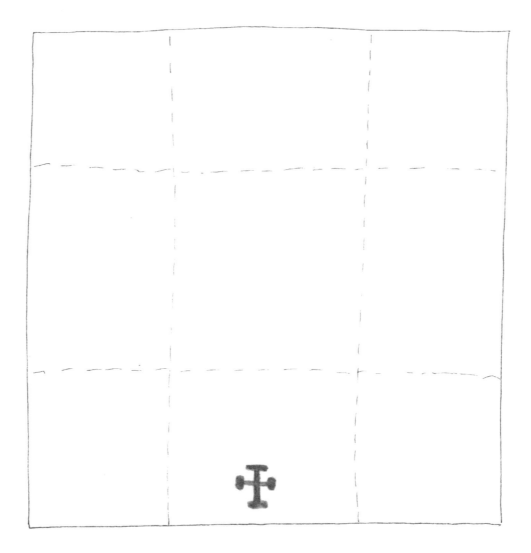

Corporal

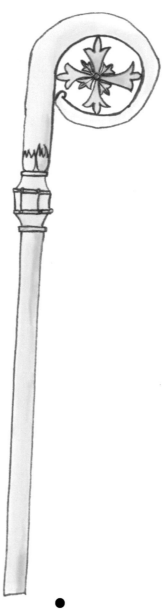

Crosier

Crucifix

Cruets

Dalmatic

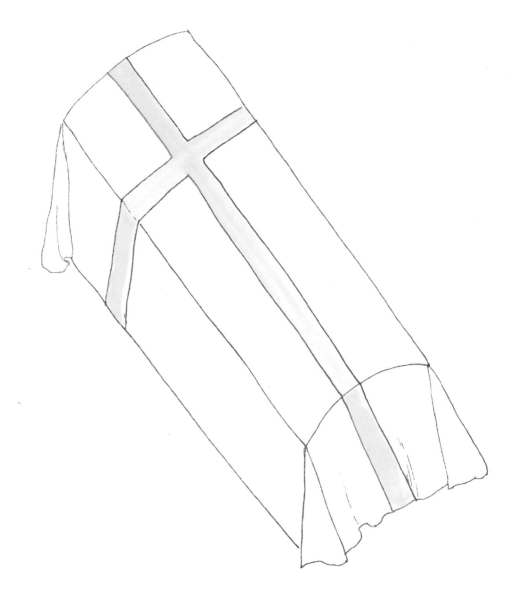

Funeral Pall

Holy Oils

Holy Water Font

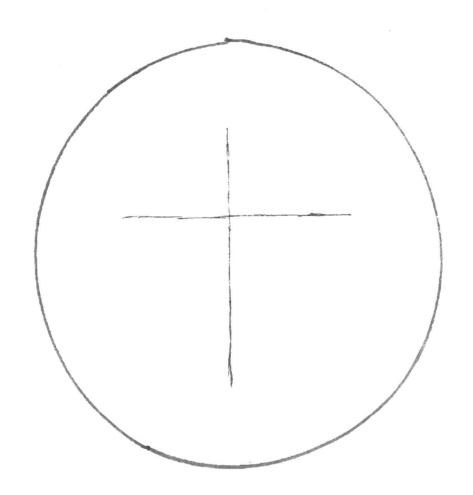

Host

Hymnal

Icon

Kneeler

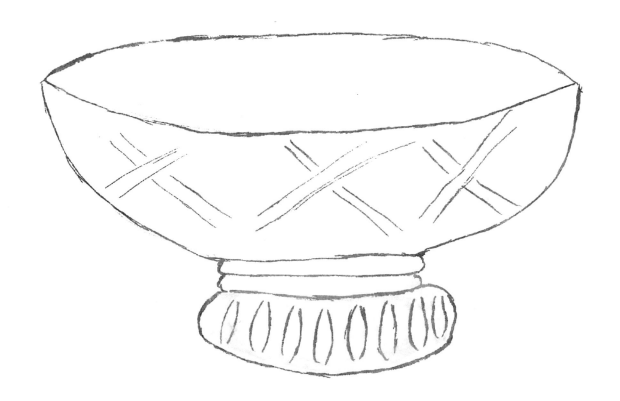

Lavabo

Lectionary

Miter

Monstrance

Nave

Organ

Paschal Candle

Paten

Pew

Presider's Chair

Processional Canopy

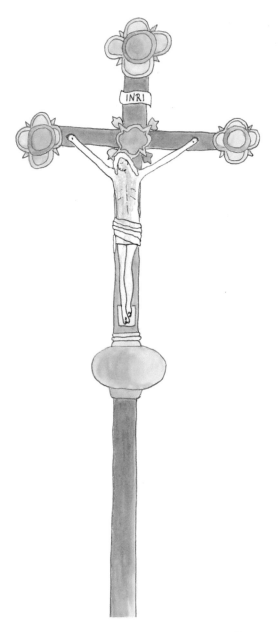

Processional Cross

Purificator

Pyx

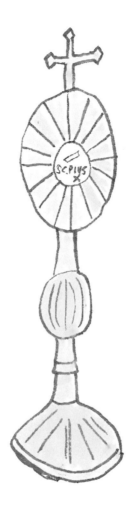

Reliquary

Roman Missal

Sacrarium

Sacristy

Sanctuary

Sanctuary Lamp

Stained Glass Window

Stations of the Cross

Statue

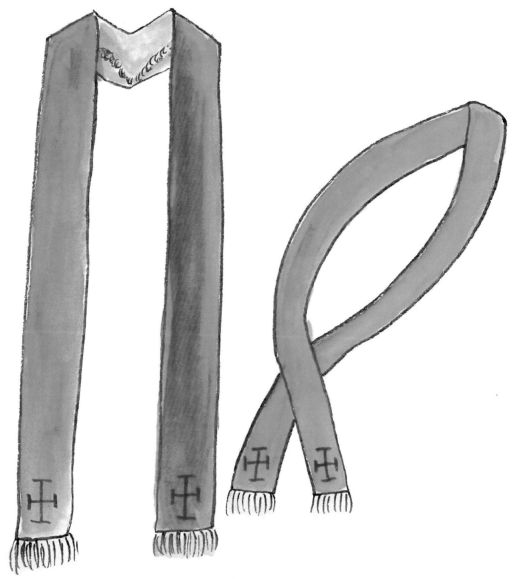

Stole

Surplice

Tabernacle

Thurible (censor) and incense boat

Vestibule

Votive Candles

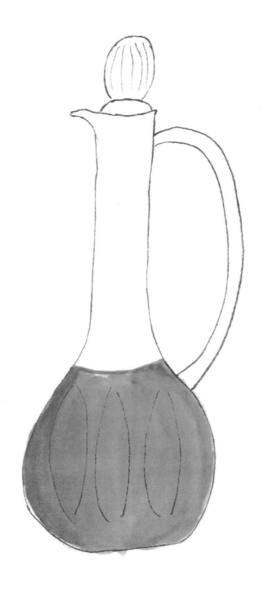

Wine

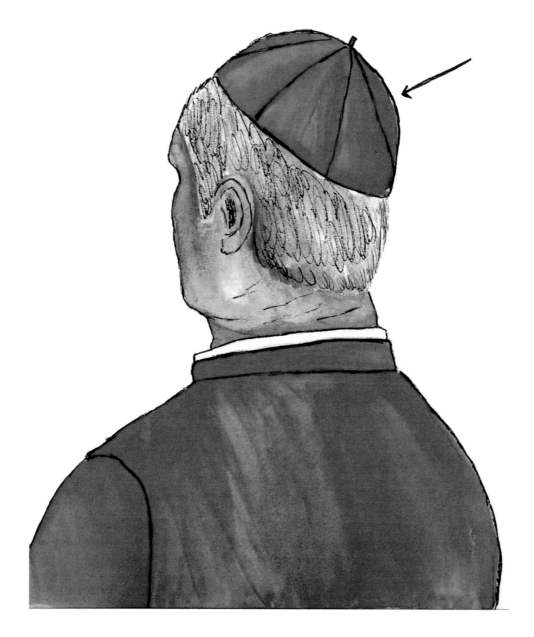

Zucchetto

88576548R00042

Made in the USA
Lexington, KY
14 May 2018